The NSA HACK AND ITS IMPLICATIONS

By Simon Luria

I0447681

Copyright information

Luria, Simon

The NSA Hack and Its Implications

–1st ed

Printed in the United States of America

Cover images : 78749703 - Big Brother
© benekamp

Book Cover Design: Simon Luria

Introduction

In my previous book, "the Panama Papers: The Largest Financial Scandal of Modern Times", the very first book on the topic, I made it clear that we are in an era of Transparency. An Era that has been ushered in by the advent of the internet. Some would say that it is a good thing; we need governments and fat cat billionaires to be more open about their dealings. On the other hand this transparency can be extremely detrimental to a nation. To have a nations secrets dumped on to the information black-market could pose risks that are far beyond any we have been exposed to before.

The spying that took place between the USSR and the United States during the cold war era pales in comparison to the spying and covert operations that are taking place now. Of course, the USSR is no more, but the ideology has lingered in the minds of those who were once members of it; old cognitive habits die hard. Vladimir Putin, the president of Russia is a cold warrior; he has made it quite clear that the cold war is , in fact, not over, it just looks very different now. In many ways, the ideologies that once clashed during the cold war are very much in place. We only need to read the headlines and we will see that the cold war between Russia and the United States has moved from outward displays of power to ones hidden behind a veil of ones and zeros.

A perfect example of this is the most recent hack of the NSA. This was by far the boldest hack in recent memory, one that has broader implications not just for the United States, but for the entire world. What we are seeing is just the very tip of the iceberg, more and more of these hacks will occur.

With these hacks, we have been ushered into a new world, a world in which the risks to our very existence will come from people living in the shadows.

Hidden In the Shadows

I have always been fascinated by hackers and hacker culture; I guess this is because when I was younger I always wanted to be one. I loved the fact that hackers are so spectral. I didn't have aspirations to hack the FBI or steal credit cards or anything like that. My ambitions were much more benign. I just wanted to have some fun screwing with peoples AOL instant message accounts and things of that nature. My skills were just adequate enough. I was considered what hackers call today A "Script Kiddie". A script Kiddie is someone who uses other people's codes to achieve certain ends because they don't quite know how to write the code themselves. That was me. I understood the codes to some degree, but in reality, I just ripped the code and tried to make it work for my own endeavors.   In this book, we will not be discussing the work of script Kiddies,but rather of those who know exactly what they are doing. Before we do that, let us touch upon pertinent background information.

What is a Hacker?

A hacker is quite simply a person who uses computers to gain unauthorized access to data that is stored on another computer or server. Often these hackers take measures to cloak their identities. Like any profession, be it a reputable or nefarious one, there are various levels of competency. In hacker culture it is no different, there are several levels of proficiency which we will touch upon briefly.

Some hackers aren't very advanced and thus aim their sights low and hack simple websites in order to use them for spam and things of that nature. Some might just do it for fun. Despite that being a rather low level hack, it can still be quite devastating to the websites of a small business or individual. Often these sites become so corrupted by these low level hacks they need to be deleted altogether and built from scratch. These hackers are truly a menace. A Script Kiddie could pull this off relatively easily.

Another kind of low level but potentially devastating hack is the DDoS or the Distributed Denial of Service attack. The goal of the DDoS is to flood a given website and server with a tremendous amount of traffic thus overwhelming their servers. This often leads a site to be unreachable because it no longer has the bandwidth to receive new visitors. In other words, DDoS causes the target website to crash. We have seen many of these attacks over the past few years. They are not complicated, but are still low level and do not need to be that complicated to execute. If a websites has adequate security measures in place, a DDoS Attack can be averted or remedied rather quickly. This type of attack can be orchestrated by a group of Script Kiddies, again, not very advanced. However, there have been several DDoS attacks that truly caused damage, but most can be averted. There are scripts (code) you can get for free or buy for pennies that will allow you to execute this kind of attack. I will not be providing those sources in this book, but they are very easy to find. A simple search online will yield many hits. **If you decide to search it, please be very** careful, many of these sites are simply fronts for hackers to get your information...*You have been warned!*

Then we have hackers that have an agenda, more commonly known as "hacktivists" such as Anonymous for example. These hacktivists run the gamut of ideology and intention. Some truly do have positive agendas such as those that disable and destroy child pornography sites or other sites that are connected to criminal activity. Then you have those who in their own mind might be doing great good, for example those who hacked Koch Industry websites, NATO, Bank of America or governmental sites. These hackers may have anti-capitalist sentiments and thus think that by hacking these organizations they are doing the world good. The USA TV series "Mr. Robot" is very much about this kind of hacker. If you have not had a chance to watch it, I highly recommend it.

Then we have hackers who just want to mess with big organizations simply to demonstrate their prowess by exposing the vulnerabilities of certain target websites and servers. A subgroup of These kinds of hackers are also in it for the sheer fun of it. For example LULZSEC or (LOLS SECURITY) are in it for shits and giggle as it were. Often they don't look for fame, they just want to expose vulnerabilities and get a good laugh at the expense of the "system". Often these are called "Black Hat Hackers". This kind of hacker is no pimply faced Script Kiddie, these people know exactly what they are doing. Unfortunately, it is this kind of hacker that can be quite a menace. LULZSEC for example is comprised of bored hackers looking for a thrill...Let me tell you, a bored hacker is a very dangerous person.

Then we have straight up gangster hacker groups. These hackers are in business solely to commit crimes. These are the ones that hack ATM machines so they spew out money without the presence of an ATM card or credit card. They are also responsible for extorting every day individuals by locking their computer and threatening to release sensitive information unless a ransom is paid. Often they use programs called "Ransomware". As of the time of this writing, these attacks are aimed at individuals but there is no doubt these programs will soon be used against large corporations. This kind of hacker is no Script Kiddie either.

The final and most dangerous form of hacker Is the one backed by a nation state. Such as hackers from China and Russia etc. These hackers are very dangerous because they have theoretically unlimited resources at their disposal. They are very capable of stealing state secrets which could lead to devastating outcomes.

It is this level of hacking that was involved in the most recent NSA hack. In the next chapter, I will discuss the NSA in general and why the hacking of the NSA is such a devastating blow to the world in general. After that, we will discuss the hack itself.

Big Brother or Concerned Father?

Ask anyone if they think the government is looking out for their own good and most will tell you they are not. Many people are inherently suspicious of the government and think that government surveillance has gotten out of control. These suspicions have been confirmed to some extent by Edward Snowden's leak of classified NSA data. This has also been demonstrated by Wikileaks as well. The NSA is in fact snooping on Americans, this we know and for some this might be very disconcerting. We must remember, however, the NSA has a broader mission in mind. Its purpose NOW is not necessarily to track those who have anti-government views, but to protect the country as a whole from major emerging threats. This is actually a good thing. No security program is going to be perfect, there will always be some collateral damage when collecting information.

When the NSA beefed up its surveillance after 9/11, it was clear some of the data collected was that of the average citizen. It's an occupational hazard. The Washington Post in the summer of 2014 showed that at least 90% of those who are placed under the watchful eye of the NSA are not necessarily the ones targeted for surveillance. So in this way, the conspiracy theorists were right to suspect this was happening.

The NSA or The National Security Agency, as the name implies, is an intelligence organization with the specific mission to keep America safe from foreign and domestic threats. This also includes threats to the technological infrastructure of the governmental

Information and communications systems. It monitors, collects and processes endless amounts of data from all across the world for intelligence and counterintelligence purposes. For the most part, it collects much of this data in a passive manner, but in many circumstances when specific information is needed, they will indeed "hack" a target, be it a nation or individual if need be. Its function is mostly technological in nature and does not rely on Human espionage like the CIA does.

The NSA was originally a division created to decipher enemy codes during the Second World War. At that time it was just an intelligence unit and not a standalone agency. In 1952, Harry S. Truman authorized that it became a formal organization under the Department of Defense. It is now one of the largest intelligence agencies in American, if not the world.

Although the NSA has always garnered suspicion from conspiracy theorists and the public in general; it was only in 2013 when it became the focus of intense media attention and what was thought of as a conspiracy theory turned out to be largely true. In that year, Edward Snowden, a contractor for the NSA leaked documents that illustrated how the NSA intercepts and processes the communications of well over a billion people globally. A sizable portion of the billion or so people are Americans. Some of the data intercepted comes from landlines, cell phones and internet traffic. Its tentacles are far-reaching in that respect. It's interesting to note that the data compiled are not exclusively used for security purposes. Some of this data is top secret economic and commercial interests of various foreign government and individuals. Another interesting thing to note from the leaks is that the NSA , or rather a unit of the NSA is responsible for locating individuals in the Middle East that are slated for assassination by the CIA. I am sure that department is quite busy.

No matter what you might think of government surveillance, we must come to terms that it is a necessary evil. We live in a very complex, interconnected world and threats loom behind every corner. As technology is advancing, so is the risk that comes with it. Gone are the days when a nation threatened nuclear war (unless you are North Korea), the new weapon now is software.

Our entire global economy and security is running off software. Your phone is running software, your computer, maybe even your watch. Even our household devices are increasingly run on software with a direct link to the internet. This may be very convenient but it is also risky. It's for this reason the NSA is working overtime to prevent foreign governments and hacktivist groups from hacking our systems and bringing down our technological infrastructure which in turn brings down the economy. In some instances such as government sponsored hacking, the intent is to wound the target, not kill it. Hostile governments know that taking down the United States would mean certain doom for them as well. Its only the hacktivists who often aim at bringing the entire system down despite the ramification. This is a scenario that unfolds in the show Mr. Robot.

We may feel overjoyed that the NSA got hacked but it has very dire implications for the world. Yes, it is ominous that the NSA keeps tabs on us, but their overarching goal is to protect the United States. If they are able to be hacked, we can expect that the hackers will eventually gain access to all parts of our technological infrastructure leading to untold damage. So although we may not like "big brother" we must assess their role with fresh eyes. Despite their reputation, we are much safer with them, than without them. I might get pilloried for saying that, but it is the truth. I will go into this further in a future chapter. Now, let us discuss the actual Hack of the NSA.

There Has Been a Breach

On August 13, 2016 news headlines across the globe proclaimed that a hacker group called the "Shadow Brokers" claimed that they hacked the NSA and lifted the very software the NSA uses to conduct hacks on other nations. In order for them to even get close to this software or code, they had to go through a group of hackers associated with the NSA called the "Equation Group". This group of hackers is considered to be the most advanced hacker group in the world. Although it has not been 100% confirmed, it is believed the Equation group works, at least in some way for and with the NSA. To get yourself past the Equation group would be an almost impossible feat.

The Shadow brokers say that they have a piece of software that for all intents and purposes is a "cyberweapon". Meaning, this application/s has the ability to cause widespread destruction to networks and systems. Some of these applications are Malware, various hacking tools and exploits used by the NSA. More specifically, the files contain various configuration files for C&C or Command-and-Control servers, various installation scripts as well as exploits that target firewalls and routers made by such companies as Fortinet, Cisco and Juniper networks to name a few. Some of the names of these applications match what Edward Snowden leaked in his own expose. Programs such as "BANANAGLEE" , "EPICBANANA", "EXTRABACON" AND "EGREGIOUSBLUNDER" to name a few. Now to be clear, the hackers didn't attack the entire NSA system but most likely just one of its Malware staging servers. These servers are as the name implies, a staging ground for the NSA to launch its own Malware attacks on selected targets.

The Shadow brokers pretended to offer this information for sale to the highest bidder. As of the time of this writing, the group asked for 568 million dollars in bitcoin to release the codes. (In all actually, I don't think this was about money at all, this was more like a PR stunt).

At first it was not clear if a hack actually took place or who was behind it. Our default reaction to hacks nowadays is that the Russians are behind it. In this instance, this may very well be true. It is now established that a hack did in fact take place, of that we are certain. Cyber security analysts from across the global are convinced these files are legitimate.

"If this is a hoax, the perpetrators put a huge amount of effort in," security researcher The Grugq told Motherboard. "The proof files look pretty legit, and they are exactly the sorts of exploits you would expect a group that targets communications infrastructure to deploy and use." --- The Hacker News.

One of the leading international software security groups **Kaspersky Lab** has confirmed that the files involved in the NSA hack contain digital signatures that match those of the "Equation Group". In their blog post "The Equation Giveaway" it states:

"While we cannot surmise the attacker's identity or motivation nor where or how this pilfered trove came to be, we can state

that several hundred tools from the leak share a strong connection with our previous findings from the Equation group,"

They go on to say:

"There are more than 300 files in the Shadow Brokers' archive which implement this specific variation of RC6 in 24 other forms," the researcher wrote. *"The chances of all these being fakes or engineered is highly unlikely."*

RC6 is an encryption algorithm used by the Equation group in some of their malware applications.

As a side note. Kaspersky Lab has tied the Equation Group to the Malware 'Stuxnet' that was used successfully **BY THE UNITED STATES** against Iran's Nuclear Turbines.

Although Kaspersky Lab is very reputable, we will need further evidence that these applications are in fact used by the NSA. Such evidence was presented in the Washington Post column "Powerful NSA Hacking Tools Have Been Revealed Online"

In the article, a former NSA employee who asked to remain anonymous came forward. He worked in a division called "Tailored Access Operations". He states, *"without a doubt, they're the keys to the kingdom... The stuff you are talking about would undermine the security of a lot of major government and corporate networks both here and abroad,"*

A second former employee of the division who had a chance to view the files stated ***"From what I saw, there was no doubt in my mind that it was legitimate."***

Now that there is reasonable certainty of the authenticity of the hack and the files involved, let us take a look at two of these exploits in brief. I won't of course reveal the codes, I did not request access to those exploits, but we do know what some of these applications do.

Examples below:

EXTRABACON Zero-Day Cisco Router Exploit:

This exploit compromises Cisco Systems firewall applications. We know this is a true exploit because Cisco confirmed as much in the security advisory section of their website. The Article is titled "Cisco Adaptive Security Appliance SNMP Remote Code Execution Vulnerability"

This exploit involves systems that are used to protect Government networks, corporate networks and data centers. So having this exploit can cause a lot of damage.

The exploit works something like this:

A zero-day vulnerability (CVE-2016-6366) accessed by the EXTRABACON exploit has the ability to allow any unauthenticated hacker to cause a reload of the system in question. This allows the hacker to take control over the device itself via remote code execution. This leads to a breach in the firewall. This could come in very handy for the NSA when it conducts its hacks.

EGREGIOUSBLUNDER Exploit:

Fortinet, another firewall company acknowledged that its system can also be exploited by the EGREGIOUSBLUNDER Exploit. The said as much on their advisory site "Cookie Parser Buffer Overflow Vulnerability"

The exploit works something like this:

As the vulnerability suggests, it is a cookie Parser Buffer exploit. A cookie parser is used to processes cookie headers, these headers are used by the HTTP state system. This is the header sent to the server. The EGREGIOUSBLUNDER exploit allows for an attacker to take over the device by sending a specific kind of HTTP request. This causes a malfunction in the parser.

As you might imagine, being able to break through the firewall of a hostile government could be of immense value for the United States Intelligence agencies.

The above, of course, is just a small sample of what these tools can do.

I suppose a few questions should be asked. Why would this group expose these files? According to their own representative it was to expose the wealthy elite. Here is an excerpt of their poorly worded statement.

"We want make sure Wealthy Elite recognizes the danger cyber weapons, this message, our auction, poses to their wealth and control. Let us spell out for Elites. Your wealth and control depends on electronic data. You see what "Equation Group" can do. You see what cryptolockers and stuxnet can do. You see free files we give for free. You see attacks on banks and SWIFT in news. Maybe there is Equation Group version of cryptolocker+stuxnet for banks and financial systems? If Equation Group lose control of cyber weapons, who else lose or find cyber weapons? If electronic data go bye bye where leave Wealthy Elites? Maybe with dumb cattle? "

It seems unlikely they are just trying to stick it to the man. We will discuss that later.

I suppose an even greater question is, who was behind this hack? We will discuss this in the next chapter.

Are Rumors Just Unconfirmed Facts?

This book would not be complete without a good dose of conspiracy theory thrown into the mix. It's practically un-American not have at least one conspiracy theory revolving around an event. This NSA hack is certainly no exception.

Many rumors are flying around, some say it was an inside job, some say it was the Russians and others think it was simply human error which allowed for the codes to be exposed by mistake.

As you may know, Edward Snowden, the NSA contractor who spilled the beans on the top secret Surveillance operations of the NSA is hiding out in Russia. For obvious reasons he cannot return to the United States since he would most likely be tried for treason. He had quite a bit to say about this most recent hack. Much of it simply confirmed what he already leaked (sans the actual computer codes) he goes a step further and states that he believes that this hack was perpetuated by Russia. He states in one of a series of tweets:

"Circumstantial evidence and conventional wisdom indicates Russian responsibility,"

Snowden is not the only one who suspects this, many cyber security experts also believe that the Shadow Brokers who stole the Equation Groups / NSA exploits are Russian in origin. This is not farfetched, it is believed that Russia has been behind quite a few recent high profile hacks such as the one against the Democratic National Committee (DNC) which exposed some pretty damning emails which led to the resignation of DNC head Debbie Wasserman Schultz.

It is also no secret that Vladimir Putin and Donald Trump, the Republican Nominee for president have a kind of Bromance from a distance. Many believe this was Vladimir's way of helping out his republican "friend".

Stewart Baker , a former NSA general counsel told NBC News states that *"the assumption that it is Russian intelligence is a good first estimate, as it's one of a half dozen leaks of information directly hostile to the U.S. government and U.S. institutions."*

It is also no secret that Vladimir Putin and Hillary Clinton despise one another. Especially Putin, he has an axe to grind. When Hillary was Secretary of State, she accused Russia of not having free elections. Putin fumed at this accusation. He accused Hillary of trying to meddle in Russian elections. Perhaps this is his way of getting revenge?

In all fairness to the Russian Intelligence agencies and Putin, there is no true smoking gun indicating Russia is behind any of these attacks. However, the circumstantial evidence is quite damning. One of the more interesting aspects about this whole story is that this group "The Shadows Brokers" did not exist prior to this hack. I looked far and wide and could not find a trace. I also find it suspect that they emerged just now. Many security analysts agree that this hack appears to be more about Russia getting back at the United States for blaming them for the DNC hack. Which if truly executed by the Russians can prove that they can meddle with our political system quite easily. Putin accused us of doing just that.

Tit for tat!

Russia has a long history of using cyberwar and attacks as a strategic weapon. In the 2008 skirmish with Georgia, they used both Cyber and conventional tactics to quell the uprising.

In December of 2015, Russia hackers brought down part of the power grid in the Ukraine. The Russian hacker threat is so real that earlier this year, Estonia drafted plans to backup its data in the UK just in case Russian hackers decided to breach their own homegrown defenses. Russia has expansionist visions for the Baltic States, Estonia, Lithuania and Latvia are certainly cyber targets for Russia.

Another high profile case of Russian hacking just occurred as I write this 8/23/2016. Over the past few months, the New York Times has been regularly hacked by Russian operatives trying to glean some kind of intelligence information from journalists. This is a smart move. Often times journalists are given classified information "off the record" for upcoming articles and in some cases they are given information that would not otherwise make it to the article, but is still stored in their notes on their computers. It was also revealed that the hackers are targeting think-tanks as well. This also makes sense since many think-tanks have some say in crafting US policy.

There are, of course, other theories such as the potential for this to be an inside job. Perhaps another Snowden at the NSA? Another theory is that the hack was in fact Russian in origin, but not necessarily government-sponsored.

We also must keep in mind that Russia is the villain of the hour for the United States and Europe and so is blamed for pretty much all hacks that occur now. When North Korea was the villain of the hour, the United States and Europe blamed them for the Sony Hack in 2014, as well as other hacks. We must keep this mind when assessing this recent hack.

Hacker identification will always remain part art-form, part science. Hackers often share tactics and codes with one another, so what may look like a Russian digital signature may very well be a North Korean one or a Chinese one. For all we know, all these hacks could be coming out of Israel. In light of this, We must keep our minds open to all possibilities.

In the end, we can't know with absolute certainty who pulled off this hack. That is the whole point really, hackers are in business to remain anonymous, they are more dangerous when they lurk in the shadows. If in fact the Russians are behind this, then we are no doubt witnessing a Cyberwar between the United States and Russia play out right before our eyes.

One of the most disturbing aspects about this Cyberwar is that the Republican Nominee for President, Donald Trump, is encouraging it further by asking Russia to find the supposed missing emails from Hillary Clinton's email server. He stated, and a I quote

"Russia, if you're listening, I hope you're able to find the 30,000 emails that are missing." In a press conference in Doral Florida he goes on to say **"If they hacked, they probably have her 33,000 emails. I hope they do,"** This is a very dangerous game he is playing. It doesn't matter if you are for Hillary or not, He is asking a hostile government to illegally "obtain" emails from an individual who was then a top-ranking cabinet member. This is bordering on Sedition and even treason.

Whether it was the Russians or not, we don't know. One thing we can know, is that this NSA hack has very broad implications for us all.

Is Any One Safe?

In light of this most recent hack and those of the past few months, is any one truly safe? If the NSA got hacked so easily, what does that say about the system as a whole? What about business both large and small?

 Business News Daily in an article "Cybersecurity: A Small Business Guide", indicated that it was of the utmost importance that companies of all sizes beef up their cybersecurity. They found that small companies are just as vulnerable to hacks as large companies are.

According to the Keeper Security and the Ponemon Institute, just about 50 percent of small businesses have been hacked in some form or another in the past 12 months. - The 2016 State of SMB Cybersecurity. That is a staggering number and it is most likely an underestimation.

Despite this, we must agree, the Internet has been an amazing tool for the human race. We do almost everything on it and with it. It has streamlined so many processes. If I were to write a piece similar to this in the 80s, it would take me months, if not years to compile the various elements from libraries across the country and even around the world. Now, I can press a button, send a few emails and viola, a book is born in a short period of time. In the 80s, if you wanted to buy furniture or clothing, you had to get up and visit several stores until you found the right item. Now, you can , in just a few clicks, get exactly what you want, at a cheaper price AND in some cases you may even get same day delivery. It is no wonder 3 billion people worldwide use the internet.

Alas, like everything it seems, there is a risk to this convenience. We are surrounded on all corners by people who want to exploit our usage of the internet. In fact, there are armies of these people just waiting for us to slip up once in order to invade our privacy, steal our identities and destroy our lives. Now imagine what these same people can do on a global scale. If they can hack the NSA which is an impenetrable fortress, just imagine. Many top security analysts state that it is only a matter of time before a widespread cyber attack will occur. Some have coined such an attack as a "Digital Pearl Harbor" or a "Cyber 9/11". Perhaps some of these individuals are taking it too far, perhaps we are immune to such widespread surprise attacks. Suffice it to say, we are still highly vulnerable and we certainly have many pain points that can be pressed.

The internet has come into our homes in ways unthinkable even just 10 years ago. The internet is no longer just some service we use to extract information on our computers, it has also become a conduit of operation for many of our household appliances and even our vehicles. The term for this internet invasion into our home lives is called "The Internet of Things". We can now set our TVs, our heating/AC units and even lock our doors via the internet. Even some pacemakers are wired to it. All you need is an app and a device that it can communicate with and you're in business. It is projected that at least 70% of all cars will be connected to the net at some point in the future.

If hackers can infiltrate the NSA, they can also infiltrate your toaster oven, unlock your doors, and drive you into a ditch. Or perhaps ransomware can be installed into a pacemaker causing the patient to be at the mercy of a hacker who demands a ransom. If the patient doesn't pay, instant heart attack. I know this sounds rather dire, but these are all very likely scenarios. That is why we need to wake up and take this NSA hack seriously.

Every day we are learning of new cyber attacks. They are only getting more prevalent. On the one hand this is good because it helps the "good guys" create more efficient security measures. However, the hackers are always a few steps ahead. That is why it is imperative that we all take the proper precautions.

I am not saying we should give up the internet or the internet of things for that matter. But we must make sure we keep these applications and devices constantly updated with the latest security patches. We all tend to ignore patch updates but often those patches are what keep us safe from vulnerabilities, even if temporarily.

Unfortunately, we can never be fully protected, the only way we can secure ourselves from future events is for a few disasters to occur first. We learn the hard way not because we don't know any better, but sometimes the hard way is the only way to learn.

Final Thoughts

Cyber threats are nothing new. For years now we have read accounts of large-scale outages due to hacker activity. So in this sense, the NSA hack did not reveal anything we did not already know to be possible. Is it a surprise however, that such sensitive information could be so readily lifted from NSA Malware staging servers. I can understand perhaps hackers getting a hold of a few emails, but this was much bigger than that. Actual cyber weapons were stolen.

I can't help but recall the whole standoff between Apple Inc and The FBI. It involved the hacking of the IPhone of the San Bernadino shooter. The FBI wanted Apple to create a backdoor hack so the phone could be accessed. Tim Cook, CEO of Apple refused and stated that if Apple creates such a backdoor it would eventually be stolen and those who steal it will use it against millions of other IPhone users. An amusing Tweet by Christopher Soghoian, a privacy researcher and activist summed it up perfectly.

"**Apple**: If we're forced to build a tool to hack iPhones, someone will steal it.

FBI: Nonsense

Russia: We just published NSA's hacking tools. "

We are in a digital age now and our personal information is under assault. It only takes a few pimply faced 15 year olds in front of a computer to hack into our most sensitive data. Privacy, even for those with deep pockets and an army of super hackers like "The Equation Group" on their side cannot be guaranteed anymore. To me, that is the broader lesson to be learned from the NSA hack. Take Heed...The Hackers are here.

Recommended Reading

Dark Territory: The Secret History of Cyber War

Fred Kaplan

The Hacked World Order: How Nations Fight, Trade, Maneuver, and Manipulate in the Digital Age

Adam Segal

NSA Secrets: Government Spying in the Internet Age - The Washington Post

Code Warriors: NSA's Codebreakers and the Secret Intelligence War Against the Soviet Union - Stephen Budiansky

Current and Upcoming Books by the Author

www.simonluria.com

Current:

The Panama Papers: The Largest Financial Scandal of Modern Times

UPCOMING:

The Self Victimization of A People: How Judaism Fosters Antisemitism

Outlaws of Islam: The Great Satan of the East

Krokodil Tears: The Drug That Could Destroy the World

The False Promise of Reward: How Society Promotes Addiction

Source Material

http://www.bankinfosecurity.com/

Were Russians Involved in NSA Hack?:

http://www.nbcnews.com/news/us-news/were-russians-involved-nsa-hack-n632666

WikiLeaks promises to release hacked NSA cyberweapons:

http://www.dailydot.com/layer8/wikileaks-equation-group-shadow-brokers/

Snowden: Alleged NSA attack is Russian warning:

http://www.cnet.com/news/snowden-nsa-hack-russia-warning-election-democratic-party/

Hackers likely stole NSA cyberweapons now what?:

http://www.dailydot.com/layer8/nsa-hack-shadow-brokers-us-response-what-next/

Cisco patches 'ExtraBacon' zero-day exploit leaked by NSA hackers:

http://www.dailydot.com/layer8/cisco-asa-nsa-shadowbroker-patch/

The NSA's website keeps crashing for unknown reasons:

http://www.dailydot.com/layer8/nsa-website-down/

Spying tools stolen in Shadow Brokers 'NSA hack' could beat firewalls says Cisco:

http://www.mirror.co.uk/tech/stolen-nsa-hack-spying-tools-8655759

Cisco, Fortinet Confirm 'NSA Hack' Vulnerabilities Exposed By 'Shadow Brokers':

http://www.techtimes.com/articles/174174/20160818/cisco-fortinet-confirm-nsa-hack-vulnerabilities-exposed-by-shadow-brokers.htm

Edward Snowden Believes Russia is to blame for a hack on the NSA: http://www.newsweek.com/snowden-russia-nsa-hack-cyber-weapon-490935

War News Updates: Is The U.S. - Russian 'Spy-War' Heating Up?:

http://warnewsupdates.blogspot.com/2016/08/is-us-russian-spy-war-heating-up.html

Here's why the supposed NSA 'hack' is unlike anything we've ever seen before - Business Insider:

http://www.businessinsider.sg/nsa-shadow-brokers-hack-weird-2016-8/

NSA Hack Traced Back To Russia?:

https://www.wochit.com/share-video/57b4770ce4b0cf2ff907e539/

Snowden: Alleged NSA attack is Russian warning:

http://www.cnet.com/uk/news/snowden-nsa-hack-russia-warning-election-democratic-party/

About The Author

Simon Luria is a writer, raised in London and now based out of New York City. Far from flying under the radar, his name is often enough to start heated debates. On the one side, his fans adore him, always with their eye on his next book. On the other side, there is a vocal group of people who loathe Simon. These people vehemently oppose everything that he says, protesting him at every turn.

For his part, Simon makes no effort to quell this distaste, never seeking out controversy but at the same time never taking any steps to avoid it either. He lets the chips fall where they may. He sees the modern world as unnecessarily sanitized and politically correct, Simon refuses to fold under pressure, sticking to his principles, always telling it like he sees it. He is known for delivering blunt, well-researched musings on finance, geopolitics, foreign policy, religion, medicine, and the state of the world. His opinions have caused him to shield his true identity. It's the only way for him to produce the work he does without fear.

www.simonluria.com

www.ingramcontent.com/pod-product-compliance
Lightning Source LLC
Chambersburg PA
CBHW070245290526
45789CB00004B/1773